ESSENTIAL TIPS

BABY CARE

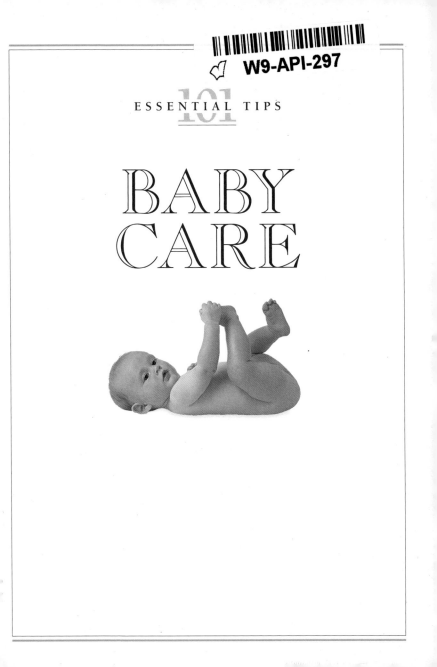

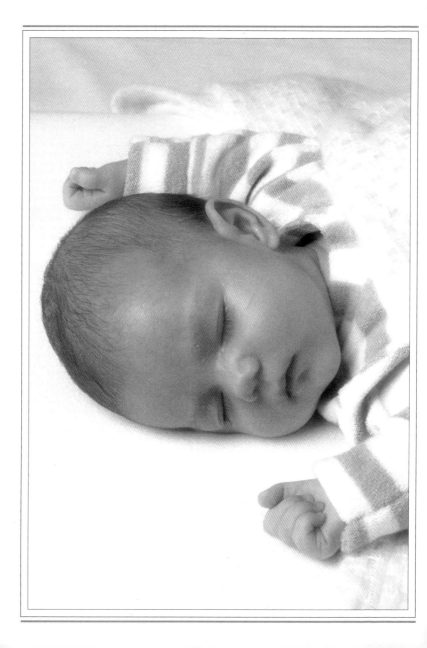

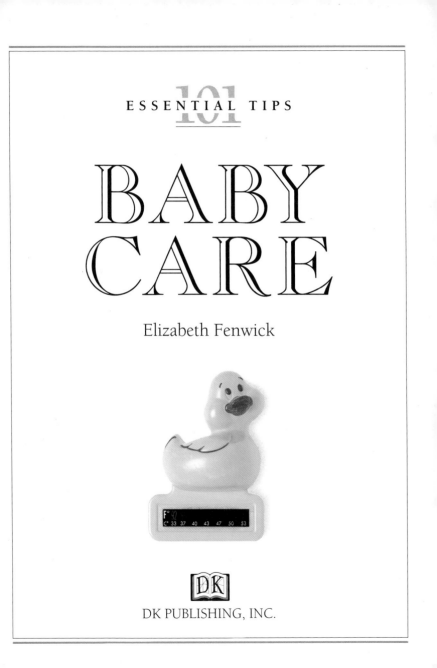

ESSENTIAL TIPS
101

BABY CARE

Elizabeth Fenwick

DK

DK PUBLISHING, INC.

A DK PUBLISHING BOOK

www.dk.com

Editor James Harrison
Art Editor Sharon Lunn
Series Editor Charlotte Davies
Series Art Editor Clive Hayball
Production Controller Lauren Britton
US Editor Laaren Brown

First American Edition, 1996
4 6 8 10 9 7 5 3

DK Publishing Inc.
95 Madison Avenue
New York, New York 10016

ISBN 0-7894-0567-9

Text film output by The Right Type, Great Britain
Reproduced by Colourscan, Singapore
Printed and bound by Graphicom, Italy

ESSENTIAL TIPS

HANDLING YOUR NEW BABY

1 PICKING UP A NEWBORN

To calm and reassure your baby, as well as yourself, make eye contact and talk soothingly to her before you pick her up. If you snatch your baby suddenly, you will startle her. Slide one hand underneath her to support her lower back and bottom. From the opposite side, slide your other hand under to support her neck and head. Take the weight of her head and body, and gently lift her into a cradling position.

THE NEED FOR YOUR SUPPORT ▷
Until your baby is at least eight weeks old, she cannot control her head or muscles, so you must take the weight of her head and body.

△ PROTECT THE HEAD FROM FLOPPING
From a cradling position (see p.9) make sure you have one hand, palm open, taking the weight of your baby's head.

2 PUTTING YOUR BABY DOWN SAFELY

Put your baby down just as you would pick her up: that is, with your whole arm supporting her spine, neck, and head. Once the pad is taking her weight, slide your nearest hand from under her bottom. Use this hand to help lift her head so you can slide out the hand still supporting her head, and lower it down gently onto the pad.

3 CRADLING A BABY THE NATURAL WAY

From the picking-up position, carefully transfer your baby's head to the crook of your slightly inclined arm (whichever you are comfortable with) or your shoulder.

Your wrist and hand encircle her back while your other arm lends extra support to her bottom and legs. Cradling this way means your baby can look and listen to you.

SHOULDER/BOTTOM HOLD
Hold her head to your shoulder, with one hand supporting her bottom.

CLASSIC CRADLE HOLD
Cradle her head in the crook of your elbow; your other arm supports the rest of her body.

BABY FACE DOWN
A baby may like being held with her chin and cheek resting on your forearm.

4 SHOULDER HUGGING

When your baby can support her head, she will enjoy the close contact of this hold, where her head nestles by your head. Her arms cling onto your clothes or by your neck. You wrap both of your arms across her legs and bottom.

SOOTHING HOLD
This is a good calming hold after boisterous play; it is also good for burping your baby (see p.43).

5 HOLD FROM THE HIP

After your baby has learned to hold her head up, she can cling onto you while sitting astride your hip. This is a great hold when you are moving around getting her feeding or clothes ready. She feels close and safe, and also has a good view.

SELF-SUPPORTING
Your baby's knees grip your hips while your arm supports her back and bottom. This also gives you the use of a free hand.

6 GIVING GENTLE SWINGS & BOUNCES

Once your baby can lift his head and has muscle control, at around four months, you can introduce some gentle physical play, such as holding him above your head, perching him high on your shoulder, or bouncing him on your knee. Avoid shaking and rough play, which can cause serious injury. Be responsive to his mood.

HIGH SWINGS ▷
Raise your baby high above your head. He will love the sensation of flying and seeing new surroundings as well as your smiling face.

Hold him firmly in your hands with your thumbs meeting in the middle

Talk and look at him while bouncing

Don't rush to raise your baby. Do it gently and you won't strain your back or startle him

BOUNCY-BOUNCY △
Lift your four-month-old baby up and down on your knees in time to a favorite rhyme. Hold his arms to stop him from jerking back.

7 USING BABY JUMPERS & BABY WALKERS

Baby jumpers are useful for supervised play. They give baby sensations of movement while giving your arms a much-needed rest. Baby walkers should not be used unsupervised; they have been the cause of injuries. Once a baby can crawl, use any mobility aid only for brief periods: he needs to explore freely!

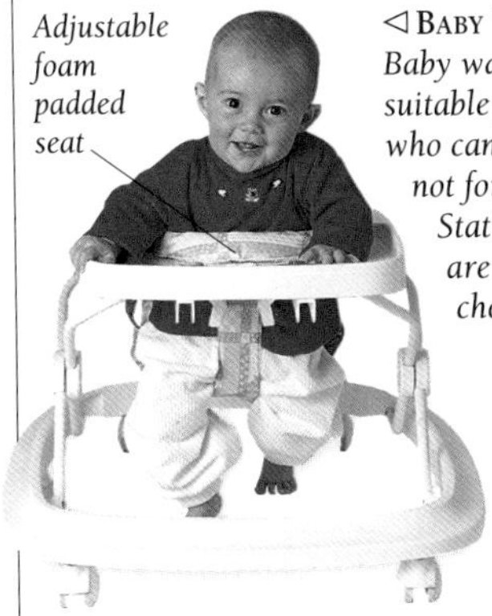

Clamps on doorway

Adjustable foam padded seat

◁ BABY WALKERS
Baby walkers are suitable for a baby who can crawl, but not for a walker. Stationary walkers are the safest choice.

BOUNCING CHAIRS ▽
From around six weeks, let your baby spend some wakeful times in a bouncing chair or rocking chair on the floor. Some have add-on head supports and clip-on toys.

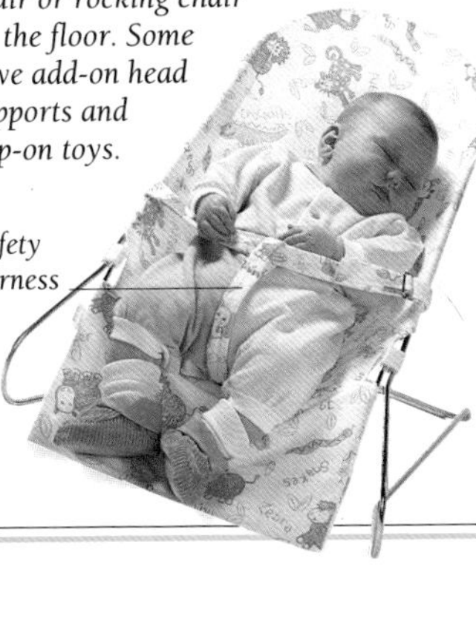

Safety harness

Toes should only just touch the floor

BABY JUMPER △
This useful playtime aid is suitable for babies from about 5 to 11 months, up to a weight of 28 lb (13 kg). A steel clamp attachment fits it onto a doorway.

8 USING A FRONT PACK

For the first three months, a front pack is an excellent way of carrying your baby around both indoors and outside. The close contact to your body and the motion as you walk soothes her, and it leaves your arms free.

Padded head support is essential

Choose a padded and machine-washable sling

Let your hands reassure your baby

1 △ Clip the belt behind your waist. If this is awkward, clip at the front and swivel it around.

2 △ Sit down with her snug on your shoulder. Keep a hand behind her and put her legs in the gaps.

3 △ Pull the straps over your shoulders. Keep one hand supporting her buttocks and back.

4 △ Sit forward, support the back of her head, and slowly let the sling take her body weight.

WELCOME TO DIAPERS

⑨ CLEANING ESSENTIALS

Changing diapers is not as daunting as it may seem, but you need to have everything ready and all within reach before you start. You must have either a changing pad or folded towel placed on the floor of a warm room (if using a changing table or bed, make sure she cannot fall off). Dispose of soiled diapers, diaper liners, cotton balls, and wipes in plastic bags; use these also to carry soiled cloth diapers. Make sure you have baby wipes, or cotton balls and a bowl of warm water, plus zinc oxide, vitamins A and D ointment, and a new, clean diaper.

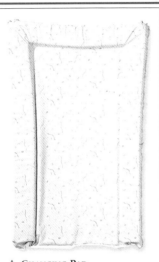

△ CHANGING PAD
Choose a padded, plastic-covered pad for easy cleaning. A towel is a warmer option for winter.

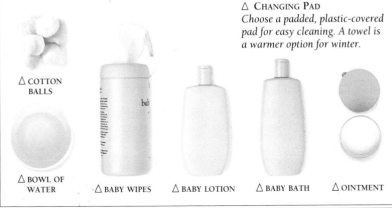

△ COTTON BALLS

△ BOWL OF WATER

·△ BABY WIPES

△ BABY LOTION

△ BABY BATH

△ OINTMENT

13

10 WHAT ARE DISPOSABLE DIAPERS?

Disposable diapers are diaper, liner, and plastic pants all in one: they allow moisture to soak through a top layer sheet into an absorbent filling, which is protected on the outside by a waterproof backing. Key features include elastic legs for a snug fit and refastenable tapes so that you can check if the diaper needs changing. Buy the correct size for your baby's weight; these are clearly shown on the packaging. They are more expensive to use than cloth diapers but are quick and easy to put on and remove, and you save on laundry time. You will be changing around ten diapers a day at first, so buy at least 70 per week.

Elastic around the legs protects against leaks

Liner draws moisture away from baby's skin

Extra absorbency at the front

BOY'S DIAPER

GIRL'S DIAPER

More padding in the center

11 DIFFERENT DISPOSABLES

Diapers come in different sizes to fit a growing baby. They range from newborn up to 10 lb (4–5 kg), right up to training pants for children. There are diapers for boys with more padding at the front, and for girls, with more padding underneath, and unisex varieties, with different absorbencies for day and night use. Choose ones with elastic waists, which help prevent moisture passing from the waist onto baby's clothing. "Ultra" diapers are slimmer and have more absorbency than the bulkier, standard diapers.

12 WHAT ARE CLOTH DIAPERS?

Cloth diapers come in bird's-eye or prefolded versions. Terry-cloth diapers are also available, or you can make your own. You will need at least 24 diapers. Buy the best you can afford as these will be more absorbent than cheaper varieties. You will also need reusable plastic pants or diaper wraps to prevent leaks. These are fairly long-term purchases, but remember there are washing costs.

◁ SAFETY PINS

◁ LINERS

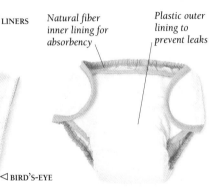

Natural fiber inner lining for absorbency

Plastic outer lining to prevent leaks

◁ BIRD'S-EYE

△ TERRY

△ TERRY AND BIRD'S-EYE DIAPERS
Terry diapers are bulkier when on than disposables, so it's advisable to buy clothes one size larger to make sure they fit. Bird's-eye is very soft and ideal for newborn babies.

REUSABLE DIAPERS △
These pants fit like disposables, with resealable tape and elastic legs, but they wash and wear like cloth diapers. Most have a waterproof backing so plastic pants are not needed.

△ TIE-ON PANTS
These tuck over the diaper around the waist and legs. They let air in but also leak.

△ DIAPER WRAPS
These come in different styles. With them, you don't have to use diaper pins.

△ PULL-ON PANTS
These reusable plastic pants prevent leaks, but can encourage diaper rash.

13 CHECKING THE DIAPER CONTENTS

Babies on milk-only diets produce very loose feces.
- For breast-fed babies, mustardy yellow, creamy stools are normal.
- With bottle-fed babies, look for pale brown, more formed and smelly stools.
- Greenish, curdlike stools are also normal for a presolids baby.
- Consult a doctor if the stools are very watery or contain blood.

14 PREVENTING DIAPER RASH

Any sign of redness (with or without spots) around the bottom area is called diaper rash. The main cause is a baby being left in a wet or soiled diaper too long. So regular checking and changing is the best prevention. Make sure you clean all the skin creases and dry completely. Allow the area to "air" without a diaper for a few minutes. Wash and rinse cloth diapers thoroughly.

15 DEALING WITH DIAPER RASH

Don't feel guilty or alarmed if your baby gets diaper rash – it's very common. At the first sign of redness change diapers more frequently. With each diaper change, use a baby wipe or damp cotton balls, and apply a layer of protective cream such as zinc oxide ointment or vitamins A and D ointment. If using cloth diapers, try using liners and avoid plastic pants.

Make sure all skin creases are clean and dry before applying cream

Diaper rash symptoms	Likely causes	What to do
■ Redness, sore-looking skin; broken skin in leg folds; smell of ammonia	■ Not allowing the skin to dry well enough	■ For all forms of diaper rash, start with careful drying. Don't use plastic pants. Allow time for a baby's bottom to dry. Don't use powder; do use a waterproof ointment or cream. If this doesn't work, see a doctor.
■ Rash starting around the front rather than the back	■ Urine breaking down into ammonia	
■ Spotty rash all over the diaper area	■ More severe form of ammonia rash	
■ Small blisters all over the diaper area	■ Heat rash from sweat in skin creases	

16 CHANGING A DISPOSABLE DIAPER

Have everything ready before you start: the changing pad, a clean diaper, cotton balls and warm water or lotion or baby wipes (for babies over six weeks), disposable bag for dirty diaper, ointment, and fresh clothes if needed. Try to make diaper changing fun. It's the perfect time for some one-to-one contact, tickles, nursery rhymes, and songs. Allow time for the cleaned diaper area to dry off naturally.

1 ▷ Once you have wiped, dried, and applied ointment, wipe your hands well on a tissue or towel as any residual cream will cause the sticky side tapes to lose their adhesiveness. Have the new diaper already opened out fully with the tapes at the top.

Have the tapes at waist height

Bring the front straight up, not twisted

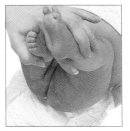

2 △ Lift your baby single-handedly by her ankles, with one finger between them. Slide the diaper top up to her waist.

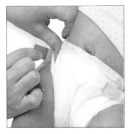

3 △ Hold one corner in position. Unpeel the tape with the other hand and pull it forward and across the front edge.

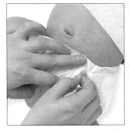

4 △ Repeat for the other side. Modern tapes allow you to unpeel and readjust to get a snug, not-too-tight fit on your baby.

17 Cleaning a Girl

First wash your hands and put your baby girl on the changing pad. Undo her clothing and open out the diaper. Wipe off the worst of the feces with a baby wipe or damp cotton balls; with a cloth diaper, use a clean corner to wipe off most of the feces. Always wipe *away* from the vaginal area toward her bottom, not the other way around. Do not try to clean inside the vaginal inner lips.

Use warm, damp cotton balls, or baby wipes

Wipe from front to back

Use free hand to keep legs from touching any feces

1 ▷ Lie your baby flat, open the diaper tabs and lift her legs using one hand (finger in between her ankles). Wipe away immediately the most obvious soiling on her body, and then slide the diaper toward you from under her.

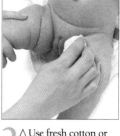

2 △ Use fresh cotton or wipes to clean inside all the skin creases at the top of her legs. Wipe downward toward her bottom.

3 △ Clean her buttocks and thighs with more cotton balls, working inward toward the anus. Keep clear of her vagina.

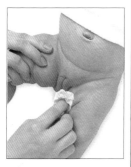

4 △ Dry the skin creases with wipes. Keep a soiled diaper open for dirty wipes. Then fold up and seal the tapes.

18 CLEANING A BOY

The same principle of wiping from the front down toward the anus (to prevent germs reaching the genitals) also applies for boys. One big difference is not to forget the small skin areas underneath the penis and below the testicles, which often harbor traces of urine or feces. Also, it is quite common for baby boys to urinate just as you remove the front of the diaper, so pause with the diaper held over the penis for a few seconds. Then open out the diaper and wipe any surface feces with wipes or cotton balls, and drop them into the diaper. Then fold the soiled diaper down under him.

1 ▽ Moisten cotton balls with water or lotion and begin by wiping his tummy across, starting at the navel. Using fresh cotton balls, or a wipe, clean the creases at the top of his legs, working down toward his back.

Wipe the creases from his front toward his back

Fold the soiled diaper under him

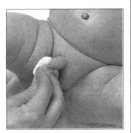

2 △ Wipe all over the testicles, holding the penis out of the way. Clean under his penis.

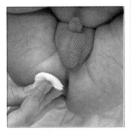

3 △ Lift his legs by the ankles and wipe outward from his anus, to buttocks, to back of thighs.

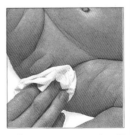

4 △ When clean, take off diaper. Dry the area and let him kick around and "air." Apply ointment.

19 PREPARING FOR POTTY TRAINING

You do not have to teach a baby bowel or bladder control. It is all part of his natural development. All you have to do is encourage him and give him the opportunity to learn when he is ready. At some time in his second year your child will start to recognize the symptoms of a full rectum and a full bladder. The next step is knowing that a movement is on the way, and once your child grasps this, he will quickly train himself to use the potty in time.

- Pick a time to learn when your child's life is free of new situations.
- Have a potty near by at all times.
- Praise him when he uses the potty successfully.
- If he has an accident, don't scold.

YOUR BABY'S POTTY ▷
Show your child how to sit on the potty. He will soon understand what it's for and be proud of himself for learning a new skill.

Pants will absorb a little urine while he learns to use a potty

If he jumps up immediately try to persuade him to stay for longer

△ TRAINING PANTS
Fabric with a waterproof backing make these pants more absorbant than ordinary ones.

20 CONSTIPATION

As your baby starts to eat a more varied diet, his stools will alter in color and consistency. Some foods can alter the color dramatically, but this does not mean that they are harming the baby. Your child will develop his own pattern of bowel movements. He may have a movement once or twice a day, or only once every two days. Whatever the pattern, do not try to alter it. Often parents think their child is constipated when he is not. A constipated child will pass stools less often and they will be hard enough to cause obvious discomfort when passed.

GOOD SOURCES OF FIBER ▷
If your child is constipated, try to include more fiber-rich foods in his diet. This will provide the bulk that helps the bowel to grip and move its contents along.

△ FRESH FRUIT
Offer your child a variety of fruits, such as slices of peeled pear, peach, and banana. They make good snacks in between meals.

△ FRESH & LIGHTLY COOKED VEGETABLES
Wash vegetables well before serving. Mashed potato and broccoli are high in fiber. Celery and carrots can be given raw.

△ DRIED FRUITS
Prunes, apricots, and other dried fruits are ideal fiber-rich treats for young children who will enjoy chewing on them.

△ WHOLEMEAL BREAD & CEREAL
Choose wholemeal rather than white bread and always pureé or mash cereal for a baby under eight months.

21 DIARRHEA

Diarrhea is the passage of very watery stools several times a day. They may look greenish and smell differently from your baby's normal stools. Diarrhea can be a serious problem for young babies because it can make them lose too much body fluid. There are a number of possible causes for mild diarrhea, but if the bowel movements return to normal after a day or two and your baby seems well and happy, there is no cause for concern.

REHYDRATION ▷
Make sure that your child has plenty to drink to replace lost liquid. A glucose drink is ideal.

22 WHEN TO CALL THE DOCTOR

If your baby has diarrhea and no other symptoms, you should contact your doctor if the diarrhea continues for more than six hours. If your baby is over a year old and seems well apart from the diarrhea you should consult your doctor if the diarrhea shows no sign of improvement after 36 hours. If, as well as having diarrhea, your baby is off his food, or is vomiting he may have gastroenteritis, a digestive tract infection that can lead to dehydration. Call your doctor if:
- Your child has a fever and/or is vomiting.
- Has blood in his stools.
- Seems lethargic or unwell.
- Shows any signs of dehydration, such as dry mouth and lips, the passage of small quantities of dark urine, not passing urine for six hours, sunken eyes, sunken fontanelle, abnormal drowsiness.

BATHING YOUR BABY

23 WHAT YOU NEED FOR BATHING

The most important piece of bathing equipment is the baby tub, which must be stable. When using a normal tub, get a nonskid mat to stop slipping. Use only baby toiletries: these are designed to be extra mild and gently moisturizing, and are hypoallergenic. Do not try to economize by buying adult shampoos, soaps, lotions, and creams. These have far too many additives and chemicals.

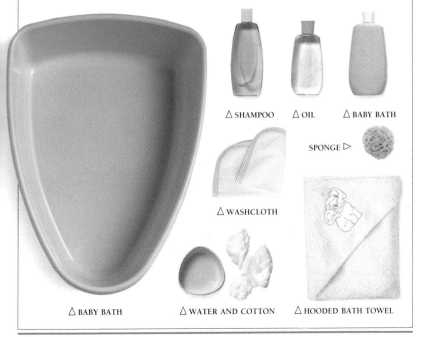

△ SHAMPOO   △ OIL   △ BABY BATH

SPONGE ▷

△ WASHCLOTH

△ BABY BATH   △ WATER AND COTTON   △ HOODED BATH TOWEL

24 BATHING & WASHING A YOUNG BABY

Bathtime should be funtime, but the first baths can seem so daunting. Your baby may dislike the first feel of water, and could even hate being naked, wet, and chilly. You may also be overanxious about dropping her. All this is perfectly normal. Apart from cleaning, your main aim is to make sure your baby doesn't catch cold. So, when washing a newborn's face, head, and hair, keep her wrapped in a towel.

Water temperature should feel warm to the elbow. With a thermometer it should read 85° F (29.4° C)

Keep eye contact at all times

Let her kick her arms and legs, feeling the splashing of the water

1 △ Pour in cold water first, then add hot water to about 4 in (10 cm) till the bath feels just warm.

2 △ Put your baby slowly in the bath, one wrist under her head, the other under her nearest thigh.

Hold her far shoulder all the time

3 △ Keep supporting her head and neck on your forearm with your hand holding her firmly around her far shoulder and upper arm. Move your other hand from under her bottom and thighs to gently splash her.

25 WASHING A BABY IN A BIG TUB

When your baby is a few months old, you can put him in a little water in the big tub. He will have more room to kick and splash around. As with a baby tub, pour cold water in first, then add hot water till it is just warm. Ensure the room is warm and everything you need is on hand. Never leave your baby in the tub or let go of him.

1 ▷ Wash his face, eyes, and ears on a changing pad first. Then gently lower him into the tub. Keep his head and shoulders supported, and ears above the waterline.

Keep eye contact and make encouraging noises to reassure him

Kneel by the tub to hold him securely

Nonskid mat already in tub

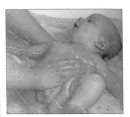

2 △ Always support him with one arm and hand. If using soap, roll it in your free hand first.

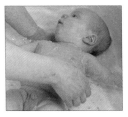

3 △ Splash water to rinse the soap off, taking care not to get it in his eyes. Talk to reassure him.

4 △ To lift out, place your hands under his armpits and hold securely but not tightly.

26 HAIR WASHING WITHOUT TEARS

You should wash your newborn baby's hair every day or two, or whenever it looks dirty. You will need hypoallergenic, no-tears baby shampoo, or extra mild bath lotion, a washcloth and a sponge. You can also buy a specially designed plastic "halo" that fits around the hairline and prevents suds from running down the face while you are rinsing the shampoo from baby's hair.

1 Use one hand to hold his head above water. Wet his hair with gentle splashes. Slide the support hand forward and put shampoo on your palm.

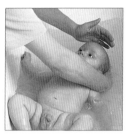

2 Swap the hand that is supporting your baby's head and gently rub in shampoo until a rich lather forms. Wait for about 15 seconds.

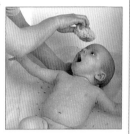

3 Swap hands again and rinse off the shampoo with a wet, squeezed-out sponge or washcloth. Wipe up and over his head, away from his eyes.

27 BATHTIME SAFETY

The most important safety feature is you: *never* leave your baby alone in the tub and always hold onto a very small or young child.
- Place a nonskid mat in the bottom of the tub to prevent slips and slides.
- Always check the water temperature first by putting in your elbow or inner side of your wrist.
- Turn off the water tightly. Even droplets can scald. Cover the hot tap with a cool washcloth.
- Never add hot water while baby is in the tub.
- Bathe your baby in a warm room.
- Keep the water heater thermostat at a moderate temperature.

△ TEMPERATURE TESTER
Use a temperature indicator strip to check for an ideal of 97–100° F (36–38° C).

28 GIVING A SPONGE BATH

Many babies hate having a bath or hate having their hair washed even if they enjoy bathtime. You can wash an older baby and avoid using a bathtub by sponge-bathing him on your lap. Start by dabbing his eyes, face, and ears with fresh, moist cotton balls. Use cool water for his face and warm water for the other parts. (*For diaper area cleaning see pp.17–19.*) Before you sit him on your lap have everything within reach.

△ **TOP HALF SPONGE**
Take off his top clothes. Wet and squeeze a sponge and wash his neck. Dry it well. Wet and squeeze the sponge again for his chest and tummy.

Wear an apron to protect your clothes

Hold arms up to flatten out skin creases

△ **LOWER HALF SPONGE**
Place a towel on your lap before you start for easy drying. Put on a clean undershirt for his washed top half, and take off his pants and socks. Wash his feet, toes, and legs, and dry off thoroughly with a towel.

△ **UNDERARM WASH**
Hold his arms up to wash his underarms where sweat and fluff gather. Wash and dry his forearms also.

29 TRIMMING BABY'S FIRST NAILS

For the first few weeks the nails are so soft that you can bite them off gently yourself. Or you can try baby nail clippers or scissors. Use whichever technique makes you less nervous. With an older baby, sit him facing forward. Hold one finger at a time and cut the nails with the scissors or clippers, following the shape of the fingertip. For toes, cut the nail straight across.

SCISSORS WITH ROUNDED ENDS

30 FIRST TEETH & GUM CARE

Once your baby has two or more teeth, wipe them and the gums every evening with a damp handkerchief. Introduce a baby-sized toothbrush at 12 months. Clean his teeth for him after breakfast and lunch. But let him play with his toothbrush at bathtime. This should take care of the first teeth. Add fun and games to brushing teeth, especially by brushing your own teeth at the same time. This will encourage your baby into the habit over time.

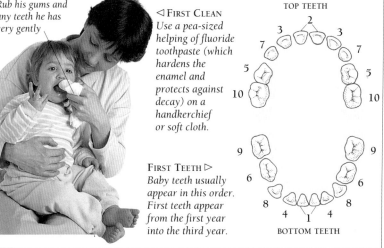

Rub his gums and any teeth he has very gently

◁ FIRST CLEAN
Use a pea-sized helping of fluoride toothpaste (which hardens the enamel and protects against decay) on a handkerchief or soft cloth.

FIRST TEETH ▷
Baby teeth usually appear in this order. First teeth appear from the first year into the third year.

TOP TEETH

BOTTOM TEETH

DRESSING & UNDRESSING

31 ESSENTIAL HOME CLOTHING

For the first six months the all-in-one stretchie, sleeper, or onesie is indispensable. Make sure these clothes are machine-washable and for daytime, are made of natural fibers to help regulate body temperature. Have at least six outfits – one on, one in the wash, one spare, and then another three. An underlayer is a must in winter.

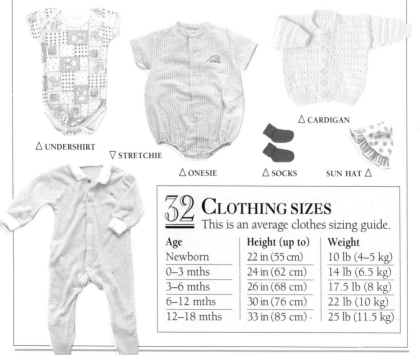

△ UNDERSHIRT

▽ STRETCHIE

△ ONESIE

△ CARDIGAN

△ SOCKS

SUN HAT △

32 CLOTHING SIZES

This is an average clothes sizing guide.

Age	Height (up to)	Weight
Newborn	22 in (55 cm)	10 lb (4–5 kg)
0–3 mths	24 in (62 cm)	14 lb (6.5 kg)
3–6 mths	26 in (68 cm)	17.5 lb (8 kg)
6–12 mths	30 in (76 cm)	22 lb (10 kg)
12–18 mths	33 in (85 cm) ·	25 lb (11.5 kg)

Stretch the undershirt with the front facing you

Lay baby on a changing pad or any nonskid surface

Check the diaper is clean

1 △ Lay baby on a flat surface. Gather the undershirt into your hands and pull the neck apart with your thumbs. Put the back edge to his crown.

33 PUT ON SHIRTS

Put on an undershirt in a warm room, away from drafts. A baby feeling the air against his skin is likely to cry; do not get flustered. Try to make this a fun time, and use eye contact and caresses to soothe him. Dressing will get easier, so be patient and gentle.

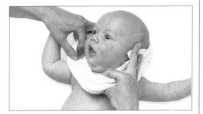

2 △ Pull the undershirt over his head, raising it slightly, and bring it down to his chin. Widen the armholes and gently guide each hand through it.

34 TAKE OFF SHIRTS

After lying him down, reach through the armhole, or sleeve, to hold one elbow inside the undershirt with one hand. Ease all the fabric over his fist. Do the same with the other elbow. Then gather up the undershirt in your hands, so there is no spare fabric that might scrape over his face. Stretch the opening as wide as you can and take it up and over his face to his crown. Slide your hands underneath his head and neck and lift his upper body to slide out the undershirt.

UNDRESS ON A FLAT SURFACE
Even if your baby can control his muscles and support his head, it is much easier to undress him on a pad than on your lap.

30

35 PUTTING ON A STRETCHIE

Have all the snaps undone. Pick your baby up and lay the clean stretchie out flat underneath him. Put him back on top of the laid-out garment. Insert the legs first, then the arms. His neck should lie just above the collar.

Garment laid out under baby in onesie

Check the toes are not snagged in the garment

1 ◁ Gather up each fabric leg and ease one foot in at a time. Place his toes right up at the end of the garment, and pull it up to his crotch.

2 △ Stretch each sleeve widely, then gather, and guide each fist through. Pull up the garment over his shoulders and do up the snaps.

Guide the hands through the tight cuffs

Pull the garment not the leg

Toes go right to the end

36 TAKING OFF A STRETCHIE

Undo the snaps first and, as you bend his leg, pull the garment away from his toes. As his leg comes out, be careful not to snag his toes. Repeat with the other leg. Put your hand inside his sleeve and hold his elbow. Grasp the cuff and pull the sleeve off, keeping his arm bent. Be careful not to catch his fingers when trying to get his hand through the cuff. Repeat with the other arm. Slide your hand under his head and neck and remove the suit.

BREAST-FEEDING

37 GETTING COMFORTABLE

Breast-feeding is absolutely natural, but it still has to be learned. Much will depend on "reading" the signals your baby gives you. But you can make things far easier by getting settled for a breast-feeding session – which could last for an hour. Lying down is ideal for nighttime feedings. For other sessions, seek good back support, such as sitting on a low chair with no arms, or lying up against a bed headboard with plenty of pillows behind you.

CROSS-LEGGED POSITION

38 GUIDING YOUR BABY TO LATCH ON

Once settled, take a deep breath and relax your shoulders. If in private, take off your top to make it easier for baby to latch on, that is, to be correctly placed on your breast, sucking efficiently. Use your baby's natural reflex to root (seek out) and to suck. If you or your baby get upset, soothe her, take another deep breath, and start again.

TRIGGERING THE ROOTING REFLEX
Stroke the cheek or corner of the mouth with a finger or nipple. This will start the baby's rooting reflex.

FINDING THE NIPPLE
Guide your breast toward baby's tongue. To "milk" your breast, the whole nipple and areola should be in his mouth.

39 MANAGING YOUR MILK FLOW

Your baby doesn't just suck, she "milks" the breast by pressing on your milk supply at the base of the areola (the colored area around the nipple). Don't worry about supply. Your baby's sucking stimulates demand. However, when your milk comes in your breasts, you may be engorged and sore for a few days. This makes the nipple flatten so it is hard for baby to latch on. Try these steps to help baby latch on and quickly relieve any engorgement.

2 △ Massage your breasts and try to express some milk (*see page 35*) to relieve them if too full.

Soften your breast with a warm washcloth

1 △ Lay a warm washcloth or warm damp towel over each breast for several minutes. You could also take a warm bath or shower to help ease the flow.

3 △ Use your free hand on your rib cage to push upward to make the nipple protrude so she can get the areola in her mouth.

40 CHANGING OVER DURING FEEDING

Let your baby suck for at least 10 to 15 minutes on one breast at each feeding. After you've burped her, or she has had a short nap, slip a finger between her jaws to break her suction, and offer her the other breast. She may be hungry enough to drain this one, too, or she may just suck for comfort. In either case, let her suck till she falls fast asleep.

41 COPING WITH LEAKING BREASTS

Your breasts may leak a lot between feeds in the early weeks. You cannot prevent this, but it will diminish as your breasts settle down and supply matches your baby's demand. To cope with this problem – and protect your clothes – wear disposable or washable breast pads inside your bra. These will absorb some of the dripping. Change the pads frequently, since wetness near your skin may make you sore.

Pads help keep your nipples dry and clean

DISPOSABLE BREAST PADS ▷
Buy shaped breast pads and be sure to wear nursing bras with wide support straps and front openings for easy access.

42 SOOTHING SORE NIPPLES

Apply calendula cream on the area

Sore, red nipples are usually the result of your baby not latching on properly. Check that she takes the whole nipple and areola area into her mouth, and that her temples and ears are moving (that is, her jaw muscles are working hard). Cracked nipples give you shooting pains during feeding, but don't stop feeding, as you may become engorged and make the problem worse.

◁ HELPFUL TREATMENTS
Apply cream or an antiseptic spray to relieve the soreness. Place a plastic breast shell to cover your nipple inside your bra to keep your breast dry. Allow it to air.

43 EXPRESSING MILK BY PUMP

Expressing with a specially made pump can be quicker and less tiring than hand expressing. Choose a syringe-type pump where the outer cylinder converts into a bottle. Soften your breasts first with warm water and massage them as if expressing by hand. The feeling on your breasts should be like your baby's jaws.

Funnel to fit over areola and nipple

Inner cylinder

Outer cylinder

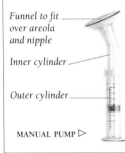

MANUAL PUMP ▷

WORKING A BREAST PUMP ▷
Place the funnel of the pump over the areola so it forms an airtight seal. Pull the outer cylinder away from you: the suction draws milk from your breast.

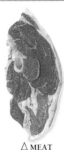

44 FOOD FOR BREAST-FEEDING MOTHERS

You will produce enough milk for your baby if you eat regularly, whenever you are hungry, drink whenever you are thirsty, and try not to become too tired. You will definitely find that you are hungrier than usual while breastfeeding – you may need as much as 800 extra calories a day. Never attempt to diet while you are breastfeeding.

△ MEAT △ CHEESE

△ NUTS

△ FRUIT LIQUID △ △ FISH

45 FIRST-YEAR FEEDING ROUTINES

How long should feeding last? How many feedings should I give my baby in 24 hours? Can I tell when she is going to be hungry? Such questions are all part of the emotional and practical worries of feeding a baby in the first year. Bear in mind the following tips when planning a feeding schudule:

- Feed your baby as often as she seems hungry, and give her as much as she wants ("feeding on demand").
- For the first month at least, do not try to establish an inflexible routine.
- If you started off in the first two weeks by feeding your newborn 10 times in 24 hours (*see chart*), this should be reduced to eight feedings, then down to six, after six more weeks.
- By two months expect to be feeding about every four hours.

- By three months plan for five daytime feedings and two night feedings.
- By four to five months plan for four feedings a day plus some solids.
- By six months your routine should be two feedings a day: early morning and bedtime.
- By nine months restrict to bedtime feeding only.
- From six months on your baby may be ready to be weaned off the breast (*see p.48*).
- If you both want to, you can continue to breast-feed well into your baby's second year or longer.
- Breast-feeding babies usually demand more feedings than bottle-fed babies as breast milk is more easily digested than formula.
- If bottle-feeding, you should be able to establish a four-hour schedule by three months.

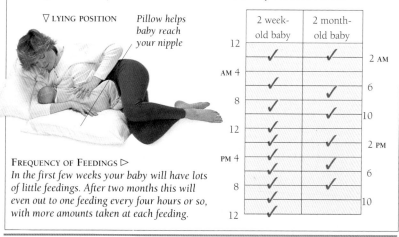

▽ LYING POSITION

Pillow helps baby reach your nipple

FREQUENCY OF FEEDINGS ▷
In the first few weeks your baby will have lots of little feedings. After two months this will even out to one feeding every four hours or so, with more amounts taken at each feeding.

	2 week-old baby	2 month-old baby	
12			
AM 4	✓	✓	2 AM
	✓		6
8	✓	✓	
	✓	✓	10
12	✓		
	✓	✓	2 PM
PM 4	✓		
	✓	✓	6
8	✓	✓	
	✓		10
12	✓		

BOTTLE-FEEDING

46 WHAT YOU NEED TO BOTTLE-FEED

To ensure that bottle-feeding is a happy experience
for you and your baby, you must be scrupulous
about hygiene, and have everything you need –
the formula, equipment, bibs, brushes, cleaners,
and sterilizers – ready in advance. Make sure
you have enough bottles, nipples, and rings to
make up bottles for a 24-hour period. To save
time, prepare all the bottles for 24 hours in
one batch and store them in a refrigerator.
Make fresh bottles when you are down to
two bottles in the refrigerator.

4 OZ (125 ML) 8 OZ (250 ML)
BOTTLE   BOTTLE

△ NATURAL-SHAPED
*The holes must face
upward so the milk
sprays over the roof
of the mouth.*

△ UNIVERSAL NIPPLE
*Flow rates vary, so
check at each feeding
for two to three drops
of milk a second.*

△ SILICONE NIPPLE
*These last up to a
year. Latex nipples
deteriorate after
about one month.*

△ STANDARD NIPPLE
*Nipples for young
babies are shorter.
Throw away worn
or bitten nipples.*

△ MEASURING
CUP

△ PLASTIC
FUNNEL

△ SCISSORS
FOR CARTONS

△ SPOON &
KNIFE

△ SALT FOR
CLEANING

47 WASHING & STERILIZING EQUIPMENT

Milk is the perfect breeding ground for bacteria, which could make your baby very ill, so keep bottles, rings, and caps scrupulously clean. Discuss sterilizing with your pediatrician; you may decide to use one of the methods shown here. All items must be washed out thoroughly using a bottle brush with warm water and dishwashing detergent, and then rinsed well. Rub the inside of nipples with salt; the scraping action will remove any trapped milk. Allow all clean items to drain on paper towels, not the drainboard. Don't warm the bottle till you need it. After each feeding, discard any milk left in the bottle.

△ BY HAND
Scrub the neck, grooves, and inside of each bottle with a bottle brush in hot, soapy water. Remove all traces of milk. Rinse well.

△ STEAM STERILIZER
Moist heat destroys harmful bacteria and cleans bottles in less than 10 minutes. The bottles do not need rinsing.

△ DISHWASHING BOTTLE-FEEDING EQUIPMENT
This is an easy way to wash your equipment, but it does not sterilize the bottle. Set the dishwasher on the hot cycle. After washing use a pin to clean the holes in the nipples.

△ BOIL TO STERILIZE
Wash the equipment, then boil for 25 minutes with everything fully submerged.

48 MANAGING A BOTTLE-FEEDING ROUTINE

Bottle-feed your baby when he seems hungry, not by the clock. Newborn babies often need as many as seven to eight meals a day, taking about 2 fl oz (50 ml) at each. So put in at least this amount of formula into each of the six bottles to begin with. By six months you will be making up 7 fl oz (200 ml) or more. As a rough guide, your baby will require about 2½ fl oz of formula per pound of body weight (or about 150 ml of formula per kg) every 24 hours. Before you begin, check the flow from the nipple (there should be several drops per second), and the heat of the formula. Try a few drops on your wrist to make sure the formula is not too hot; it should be at room temperature. Do not use a microwave to warm baby formula; it can create "hot spots" that cause severe burns in the baby's mouth. As your baby grows older, the routine will alter (*see chart below*).

MEASURING ▷
If you do not want to mix the formula directly in the bottle, or if you use disposable liners, you will need a measuring cup.

Type of milk		Birth	6 mths	9 mths	12 mths	18 mths
Infant formula	This is cow's milk modified to resemble human milk. Your baby may need vitamin and mineral supplements. Ask your pediatrician.	──────────────────▶				
Older baby formula	Also modified cow's milk intended for babies of 6–12 months or over. Vitamin and mineral supplements will be needed.			──────────▶		
Whole cow's milk	Begin this at 12 months. Supplemental vitamins and minerals also needed. Part of a preschool diet.				──────▶	

49 MIXING POWDERED FORMULA

Powdered baby formula usually comes in large cans; you scoop out the powder and mix as needed. You will need to have at least one made-up bottle in the refrigerator ready as needed. Mix following the instructions on the can exactly. You can do one bottle, or a batch of bottles, at a time, whichever is more convenient for you. Use the measuring scoop from the formula can, and use loosely filled scoops to add to each measure of water as directed. Always use fresh cold water, boiled, and cooled once, or use bottled water. You can mix the formula directly into the bottle (not the disposable kind), or via a measuring cup. Once poured, seal the bottle with the disk and ring, but not the nipple, and shake well to mix.

Hold the bottle at eye level to check you have the correct fluid level required

2 △ Open the can. Use the scoop inside to take a scoopful of powder. Level off with the back of a knife.

3 △ Do not pack the powder. Drop in each scoop. The powder should quickly dissolve.

1 △ Rinse your equipment, drain, and clean your hands. Fill a kettle or pot with fresh water and boil. Pour the boiled water into the bottles, filling them to the correct level for your measure.

50 STORING MILK CORRECTLY

Once the formula is mixed and shaken, take the disk and ring off the bottle. Put the nipple in upside down, but don't let it dip in the milk – empty some out if necessary. Reseal the disk and ring. Fill all the bottles and put the caps on. Store them in the refrigerator, ideally on a tray so that they don't fall over, and not inside the door. Do not store for longer than the can label advises.

Don't let the upside-down nipple touch the milk

51 GETTING THE BOTTLE READY

For each feeding, take the bottle from the refrigerator and turn the nipple the right way up. Warm the bottle in warm water, or at least bring it up to room temperature. Never warm the bottle in a microwave oven because the milk may get dangerously hot.

1 △ Place the bottle right side up in a bowl of warm water, or under a hot tap, shaking it all the time.

2 △ Check the milk flow to see if you are getting two or three drops per second. If the nipple isn't right, change it.

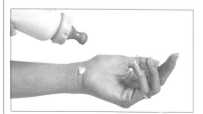

3 △ Test the temperature of the milk by shaking a few drops on your wrist. It should feel tepid but cold milk is safe too.

4 △ To keep the flow going, screw the ring so it is just on the bottle. This allows air in as your baby sucks milk out.

52 GIVING A BOTTLE

The beauty of bottle feeding is that it allows the mother some time off from the relentless feeding duties, and gives father and baby an ideal time to cuddle and bond together. Whoever is giving the bottle – parent, baby-sitter, or grandparent – needs to hold her close and talk and smile at her. Put a bib on her. Lie her half-sitting, cradled in the crook of one arm, your hand supporting her buttocks and legs. Stroke her near cheek, which should start the sucking reflex. Give her the nipple.

HOLD BABY SEMI-UPRIGHT

53 WHEN YOUR BABY WON'T LET GO

When your baby has finished drinking the milk, pull the bottle firmly away. If she still wants to suck, offer her your clean little finger. However, if she doesn't want to let go of the bottle, slide your little finger between her gums and alongside the nipple. This will break the suction.

PUT LITTLE FINGER IN CORNER OF MOUTH

54 SLEEPING DURING A FEEDING

If your baby dozes off during a feeding, she may have gas that is making her feel full. Sit her more upright and burp her (*see opposite*) for a couple of minutes. Then offer her more milk. Remember to tilt the bottle at an angle so that the nipple is full of milk, not air. She'll decide when she's had enough.

REMOVE THE NIPPLE & WAKE HER

55 SWITCHING FROM BREAST TO BOTTLE

Even if you want to bottle-feed, breast-feeding your baby for at least two days will give him valuable antibodies to help fight infection. You can then switch from breast to bottle if you decide not to continue. But if you start by bottle-feeding, you cannot then switch to breast-feeding.

If you do change over, give your baby time to adjust. Replace a lunchtime breast-feeding first with a bottle every third day. Moisten the nipple with a few drops of breast milk to help. After three days, swap a second daytime feed; then three days later a third; and finally the nighttime feed.

56 BURPING YOUR BABY

Allow your baby the chance to burp up any swallowed air, or "gas." That air may make her feel full. If she doesn't burp after 30 seconds, don't worry: it's still good for both of you to pause, relax, and slow down at a meal.

Rub her back to encourage a burp

Have a clean cloth diaper on your shoulder

△ BURPING A NEWBORN
Put a very young baby against your shoulder, supporting her floppy head under your chin. She may well bring up some milk.

△ FORWARD LEAN
Place her leaning forward on your lap. Jiggle slightly and rub her back.

◁ ACROSS THE LAP
Support your baby on your lap face down. Rub her back rhythmically.

43

FIRST MEALTIMES

57 FIRST UTENSILS & BIBS

For first meals buy an unbreakable baby bowl, spoon, and sippy cup. Start with baby spoons that have long handles and small, shallow, plastic-coated recesses so they will not hurt baby's mouth. Buy a bowl with a suction-cup bottom to stop baby knocking it off the tray. Some also come with a useful storage lid. Also handy are small plastic containers with lids suitable for storing home-prepared food in the refrigerator or freezer. A plastic juice box holder helps prevent spills if baby drinks from a carton. Always have two sippy cups: one for home use, and one that seals for travel. Buy several terry cloth bibs with plastic backing, an apron bib, and a plastic bib with tray. You also need a hand-held blender, and coarse grater to purée table food.

△ PLASTIC BOWL

△ FIRST SPOON

△ TWO-HANDED & NO-HANDLE PLASTIC SIPPY CUP

△ PLASTIC BIB

△ FOOD PROCESSOR

△ APRON BIB

△ FABRIC BIB

58 HIGHCHAIR HINTS

Once baby is sitting up you will need a highchair. Make sure it is sturdy and easy to clean. Natural wood or reinforced plastic are fine. Your choice should have a detachable plastic tray that can be opened with one hand. The tray must be large and have a rim. Check for a firmly attached safety strap with integral crotch strap.

FOLDAWAY ▷
Chairs that fold away compactly are very handy if space is tight.

Integral crotch strap for safety

Padded seat with steel frame support

△ TABLE SEAT
Ideal for traveling, this seat can be securely attached to a table top.

Sturdy pine legs that fold away after use

FOLDING HIGHCHAIR

59 FIRST FOODS FOR 4–6 MONTH-OLDS

Introduce solids when your baby is not too hungry or tired, and you are relaxed. Start with rice cereal mixed with breast milk or formula, or cooled boiled water, to make it smooth and wet and easy to digest. Puréed carrot, apple, or potato, moistened with the same liquids, without any lumps, is ideal at this stage. Peel vegetables and fruit carefully, and remove all pips. Then steam or boil, purée or sieve.

| SEMILIQUID RICE | PURÉED CARROT | PURÉED APPLE | PURÉED POTATO |

60 FIRST FOODS FOR 6 TO 8 MONTH-OLDS

Stick to fresh foods that can be mashed or minced to the texture of smooth cottage cheese. Add liquid or yogurt to help you to achieve this texture. Peel fruit or vegetables carefully, removing any pits and strings. Trim off fat and skin from fish or meat, and grill or poach, where possible. Remove any bones and mince finely. If in doubt, discuss new foods and problems with your pediatrician.

△ FIRST FINGER FOODS
Shapes made from cheese or banana, and some bread, are ideal to suck and eat.

MINCED CHICKEN   MINCED FISH   MASHED BOILED EGG

61 FIRST FOODS FOR 8 TO 9 MONTH-OLDS

You can now introduce chunkier textures, so try chopping food rather than mashing. Cook and prepare food as for a younger baby. Include foods such as toast, homemade lasagne, chopped-up chicken, and soups. Keep giving plenty of finger foods.

MASHED LENTILS   RICE

△ MORE FINGER FOODS
Cut sticks and shapes from carrots and celery as well as slices from apple, avocado, peach, and apricot to offer your baby different textures and flavors. Steam firmer fruits and vegetables.

PASTA   GROUND BEEF

62 FIRST FOODS FOR 10 TO 12 MONTH-OLDS

At this stage your baby can progress to what the rest of the family is eating, but chopped up into bite-sized pieces. Keep salt out of the diet (add table salt to your own plate if needed). Introduce stews, well-cooked pork, and steamed broccoli and cabbage as part of the diet. Canned tuna, drained and flaked, is also suitable. You can also try out fruits such as oranges and raspberries.

BROCCOLI

CHOPPED CHICKEN

GREEN BEANS

CANNED TUNA

NEW FRUITS

63 FOODS TO AVOID

Do not give whole egg before eight months (egg yolk is fine from six months). Make sure eggs are fresh and fully cooked. Spinach, turnip, and beet should not be given to babies under six months. Avoid salty, fatty, and sugary foods. Use sugar sparingly. Lowfat milk is not suitable for children under two, and nonfat (skim) milk is unsuitable before five years. Don't give peanuts to a baby or a preschool child.

AVOID NUTS: BABIES CAN CHOKE ON THEM

64 SPOON-FEEDING

To start a baby getting used to the *idea* of spoon-feeding, give her a teaspoon or plastic weaning spoon of baby food between two halves of her bottle- or breast-feeding. Holding her on your lap, put the tip of the spoon between her lips so she can suck the food off. Do not push it in. Be prepared for the mess she will make!

COAT THE TIP OF THE SPOON WITH FOOD

65 PLANNING WEANING

The time to plan dropping milk feedings is when your baby is taking solids quite happily, *and* is still feeding from the breast or bottle. Start by missing out the midday feeding when your baby is more alert and less in need of "comfort feeding." Though your baby may enjoy finger foods and cereals, she still has a basic need to suck. Give food and drink but do not offer the breast or bottle at this feeding. Do not force the process, but give it a try each day and eventually the weaning will work. Babies more than 12 months old can be given pasteurized cow's milk, or "follow-up" formula.

Timing	Solids/Drinks to introduce	6am	8am	1pm	4pm	6pm
Start	Give small tastes of fruit, vegetables, or baby cereal halfway through breast or bottle feedings.	o	o	o●/o	o	o
After 2½ weeks	Give cereal at breakfast halfway through feeding. Increase lunch solids to 3–4 teaspoonfuls. Try diluted fruit juice.	o	o●/o	o●/o	o	o
After 4 weeks	Try solids at dinnertime, halfway through feeding. Offer two courses at lunch: 2–3 teaspoons of vegetables, then 2–3 of fruit. Bring in a sippy cup.		o●/o	o●/●o	o●/o	o
After 6 weeks	Offer solids for lunch with a little milk from breast or bottle. Add a banana at snacktime; 5 or 6 tablespoons of solids per meal.		o●/o	●●/o	o●/●o	o
After 8 wks	Offer formula at lunch after solids.		o●/o	●●	o●/o	o
After 10 weeks	Give formula in a sippy cup except at breakfast. Drop afternoon feeding. Give fluids at other times.		o●	●●	●●	o
After 12 wks	Drink at breakfast. Three meals a day, plus formula.		●	●●	●●	o

● = Solids   o = Milk or Formula

66 READY-TO-EAT BABY FOODS

Commercial baby foods are fine when you cannot make fresh. Read the label first since many different types are made for each stage of weaning. Read labels and avoid preservatives, artificial flavors, colors, and added sugar or salt. Do not feed straight from the jar. Once open, cover uneaten food and store in the fridge. Use in 24 hours.

BABY FOOD

67 HELPING A BABY FEED HERSELF

By about seven months your baby will be making a determined effort to feed herself. Assist her by continuing to feed her yourself, but let her play with her food. Have a warm washcloth handy, and face the fact that most mealtimes involve a great deal of mess. Then you can show your baby how to handle a spoon and get food in her mouth rather than smear it all over her face. Be patient with her, and allow yourself the time to make this a fun as well as a learning experience. Coordination will develop gradually.

1 Spoon-feed her first, keeping the bowl out of reach. Then let her play with the remaining food while still feeding her.

2 Let her dip her fingers in the bowl and push food into her mouth. Finger foods are less messy at this stage.

3 Hold a sippy cup for her, but fill a spoon that she can pick up and hold herself. Have a clean spoon ready.

68 CHECKING THE AMOUNTS

Your baby will let you know how much she wants at each meal; but at early feedings it's best to start with about four tablespoons of food in a bowl. Do not expect her to clean her plate, but offer more if she wants it. Some days she will eat huge amounts and at other times she may eat very little. Do not worry about this as long as she gains weight.

69 FEEDING PICKY EATERS

First solids should be bland, smooth, and very liquid so they can be sucked from the spoon. Offer one new food at a time on the tip of a clean spoon before or during a feeding. Don't worry if she only seems to eat certain things; fads tend to pass after a couple of weeks. Try alternative approaches such as liquidized vegetables in soups if she won't eat them on their own.

OUT & ABOUT WITH YOUR BABY

70 CHOOSING THE RIGHT OUTDOOR CLOTHING

Babies lose heat rapidly, so in cold weather dress your baby in a padded, water- and windproof all-in-one snowsuit. To keep heat from escaping through his head, hands, and feet, put on mittens, booties, and a hat. Underneath he should wear a stretchie, undershirt, and socks, as well as a cotton or acrylic sweater on top.

△ FABRIC BOOTIES

△ COTTON/ACRYLIC SWEATER

△ TIE-ON MITTENS

△ WARM HAT

△ KNITTED SCARF

▽ WET WEATHER BOOTS

△ SNOWSUIT

71 COPING WITH CHILLING

Look out for telltale signs that your baby is too cold: crying and restless behavior, along with cold hands and feet, are the first signs of body heat loss. Warm your baby up by taking her into a heated room and hold her. Take her temperature (see p.64). If it is below 95° F (35° C), call the doctor.

72 CHOOSING A STROLLER

A traditional carriage is great for a young baby as it protects from drafts and fumes, and allows your baby to lie flat. If you opt for a stroller that folds flat for easier transportation, make sure the seat reclines fully. From three months on, a rigid-backed stroller is fine. Umbrella strollers are not suitable for babies under six months.

BASSINET ▷
Suitable from birth to six months. It can be used as a bed for the first few months, too. Fits onto chassis to create a carriage.

STROLLER ▽
Only models with full reclining seats are suitable from birth. The adjustable seat can face you or away from you.

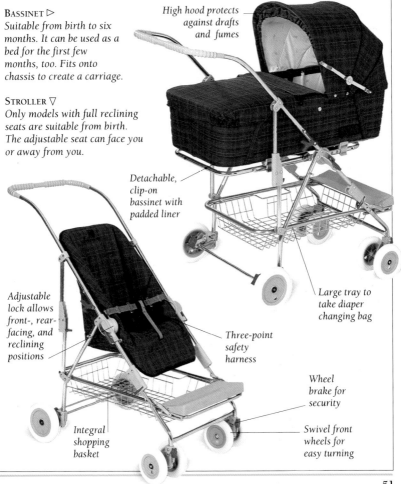

High hood protects against drafts and fumes

Detachable, clip-on bassinet with padded liner

Adjustable lock allows front-, rear-facing, and reclining positions

Three-point safety harness

Large tray to take diaper changing bag

Wheel brake for security

Integral shopping basket

Swivel front wheels for easy turning

73 CHOOSING A BABY CAR SEAT

You will probably need two different types of car seat in your baby's first two years, depending on his height and size. Rearward facing seats in the front or rear of your car are for babies up to 20 lb (9 kg). They have an integrated harness with crotch strap for protection. Forward facing seats with a five-point harness are suitable for babies from 20–40 lb (9–18 kg). You can also buy combined types.

Upright to reclining position, and washable cover

High back with molded sides to support baby and toddler

Adjustable five-point harness

△ INFANT SEAT
Rear-facing seats can be secured with an approved lap and shoulder seat belt in a back seat. Many come with a built-in handle for easy lifting when baby is asleep. Do not use these seats in passenger seats with air bags.

◁ TODDLER SEAT
These are heavy chairs to reflect the growing weight and size of your baby. They have built-up side wings for extra protection. Secured correctly, they can be used in either the front or back seat.

74 IN-CAR SAFETY ESSENTIALS

Always bear in mind the following safety tips when driving.
- Never allow a baby or young child to travel unrestrained in the car, however short the journey.
- Provide a head support cushion for an infant seat, which your

baby will need for a few months.
- Never buy or use a secondhand car seat unless you are sure of its service history. If the seat has been in an accident, the protective structure may be invisibly and dangerously damaged.

75 WHAT TO TAKE IN A DIAPER BAG

A diaper bag with detachable or fold-out changing pad is a must for any excursions outside of the home. Make sure the bag has an adjustable shoulder strap and handle for ease of carrying; or you can use a backpack. Before buying, check that the bag has elasticated internal pockets to separate diaper-changing items from spare clothes, bibs, and feeding items. Make sure you pack a few spare disposable diapers, plastic bags for soiled or wet diapers, baby wipes, lotion, a sippy cup, ready-to-eat solid food, spoons, a container of diluted juice, and also a favorite board book and cuddly toy.

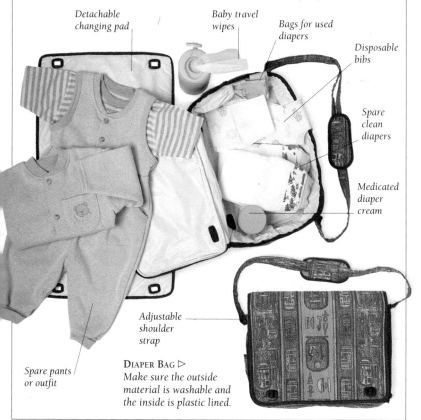

Detachable changing pad

Baby travel wipes

Bags for used diapers

Disposable bibs

Spare clean diapers

Medicated diaper cream

Adjustable shoulder strap

Spare pants or outfit

DIAPER BAG ▷
Make sure the outside material is washable and the inside is plastic lined.

76 BACKPACKING YOUR BABY

The beauty of a baby backpack is the freedom it gives you to move unhindered with your baby along busy urban streets or over country fields and pathways. The close contact reassures your baby, he gets a great view, and your hands are free. Backpack carriers are suitable when your baby can hold his head up. Many have an attached storage bag, and some brands offer an add-on rain hood.

Padded head and back rest

Lightweight but sturdy frame support

Hip belt and lumbar support

◁ BACKPACK
Look for a padded head support and shoulder straps. A freestanding frame is handy.

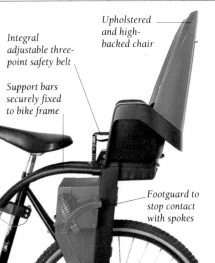

Upholstered and high-backed chair

Integral adjustable three-point safety belt

Support bars securely fixed to bike frame

Footguard to stop contact with spokes

77 SAFE CYCLING

Cycling with your baby provides all sorts of short trip opportunities without the trouble of a stroller or car. But safety and comfort for your baby must be paramount. Harnesses and a helmet are musts. Seats are ideal from 9 months up to six years (or around 45 lb / 20 kg, depending on the make). Remember that your bike will react differently with the extra weight of seat and baby.

BABY ▷
SAFETY
HELMET

SLEEPING & COMFORT

78 CHOOSING CRIBS

When choosing a crib, make sure it is made of natural wood, is covered with non-toxic paint, has a drop-side mechanism that is secure against baby handling, has bars that are no more than 2½ in (6 cm) apart, so baby cannot get his head trapped between them, and has no sharp edges. Many models have two or three mattress positions: high for newborn babies and low for older, more active babies.

△ MOSES BASKET

Sand down any sharp edges

Gaps of about 1–2½ in (2.5–6 cm)

Babyproof drop-side mechanism

Some drop-sides have safety locks

FIRST CRIB ▷

Bumpers protect against head bumps

79 COVERING UP

Your baby should be warm in bed but not hot. Buy a room thermometer and maintain an ideal temperature of 65° F (18° C). At that temperature your baby needs a sheet and three layers of blankets, or sheet and thermal blanket. Turn the sheet down over the top edge of the blanket or quilt, and tuck in around mattress edges. If too cold or hot, add or take away a layer to keep a flow of air.

80 LISTENING IN

Baby monitors allow you to relax or do the chores at home while baby is asleep. They plug into wall sockets. They pick up any sounds. Look for "listeners" with power-on indicators, preset volume safety minimum, and a built-in comfort light. The newest models come with video screens.

BABY MONITOR

MOBILE TO CATCH THE EYE

81 STIMULATING & SOOTHING CRIB TOYS

Put mobiles and colorful crib toys above and around your baby's crib. Such toys help stimulate even the youngest baby's interest in the world about him. They encourage shape and color recognition as well as looking skills. But remember a baby can only focus on things around 8 to 12 in (20 to 30 cm) away. Remove the mobiles when your baby can pull himself up to a standing position.

82 SOUND STEPS FOR A SOUND SLEEP

The most important thing you can do is ensure that your baby goes to sleep on her back.
- Relax your baby with a gentle bath and some reading time.
- Ensure the room temperature is warm, about 65° F (18° C).

- Don't smoke in the baby's room.
- Make sure that you put your baby to bed in a clean diaper.
- Before leaving the room, check she is breathing regularly.
- Make sure that the baby monitor is on before leaving the room.

83 HOW MUCH WILL MY BABY SLEEP?

At first your baby will sleep in short bursts at any time, day or night. In the next months her longest sleep will coincide more with nighttime and her wakeful periods will extend in the daytime. From six months on bedtime, from bath to sleep, is an important ritual. Daytime naps should not last more than two hours.

Age of baby	Night-time						Daytime														Night		
	1	2	3	4	5	6	7	8	9	10	11	12	1	2	3	4	5	6	7	8	9	10	11
1 month																							
3 months																							
6 months																							
12 months																							
18 months																							

■ Night time sleep ■ Daytime sleep

84 SETTLING YOUR BABY

Dress your baby for bed in a stretchie or sleeper to allow easy access for diaper changing during the night. In very warm weather an undershirt and diaper is sufficient. Give him a comfort suck of the breast or bottle if he wants one. Darken the room if necessary to create a soothing environment. An older baby may climb out from under the blankets and lie on top, falling asleep sideways across the crib. He can get his arms stuck in the bars and cry to be freed. To avoid this, try placing him halfway down the crib so that he is less likely to throw off his covers.

SAFE SLEEPING ▷
Medical evidence shows that the safest way for a baby to sleep is on his back. Most countries now follow this practice.

85 SETTLING A BABY FOR SLEEP

A younger baby will often fall asleep while sucking. (Don't put the baby to bed with a bottle – it's bad for her teeth.) But there will be many occasions when she needs you to help her relax. After six months you will need to establish a settling-for-sleep routine because she won't be so ready to go to sleep. This "routine" should be a time of fun and intimacy, but with clear signposts that your baby will come to associate with bedtime – bathing, drying, changing into a sleeper or pajamas, play and reading time, and finally putting to bed using soothing contact, gentle rocking, nursery rhymes, and lullabies.

△ CUDDLES AND LULLABIES
Rub her tummy rhythmically and sing gently to her until her eyelids close.

Push to and fro with gentle words and songs

Body contact is a great calmer

△ SOOTHING SUCKING
Up to three months, let her suck your clean little finger or a pacifier, to help her soothe herself.

◁ RHYTHMIC MOVEMENTS
Keep her in her bassinet and use its smooth, swaying motion to send your baby to sleep.

86 TAKING A BABY INTO BED

When your baby is young and still breast- or bottle-feeding, it is perfectly okay to take her into your bed (except a waterbed). Night feedings are easier if you do, and there is no risk of crushing her, provided neither you nor your partner are intoxicated. Of course it can become a habit, so you must set the limits before the habit sets in, and certainly by the time of weaning (*see p.48*).

87 COPING WITH AN EARLY RISER

Early morning waking is actually a sign that your baby has had enough sleep – even if that doesn't help you much! Leave some toys in her crib overnight for when she wakes, plus water in a nonspill cup as babies are very often thirsty when they wake. A change of diaper may give you extra rest time. These aids may keep her soothed and prevent her from crying or whimpering for attention.

88 ESTABLISHING A BEDTIME ROUTINE

Sooner rather than later you must establish a going-to-bed pattern that your baby gets familiar with and accepts. It's up to you and your partner to choose a bedtime that fits in with your own routine – late enough so you're both home, but not so late that baby is beyond soothing and the routine takes up all evening. Anytime from 6 to 8 PM is fine. Whatever you include in your baby's bedtime routine, share it with your partner.

READING A STORY ▷
Storytelling and involving her with board books are great ways of helping your baby unwind. This is a time for bonding and for prompting and responding to her reactions.

89 WAKING FOR A FEEDING

Even after six months, when a baby no longer needs a night feeding, she may continue waking for one. First ensure that she does not fall asleep at her bedtime feeding. She needs to learn to fall asleep without relying on sucking. For a few nights she may cry for a long time, but eventually she will sleep through.

△ NIGHT FEEDINGS
Resist comforting your baby to sleep with a feed. For a few nights she may cry for a long time, but eventually she will sleep

90 OVERCOMING NIGHT WAKING

Reassurance is the key word when overcoming baby's sleep problems. If he whimpers, wait a few minutes before going to him. If he cries, pick him up and soothe him. If he calms down to sniffles, put him back in his crib. Go back to bed. If he cries again, call from the bed to reassure him. Wait five minutes before going to him. This time just pat and rub his back. Tuck him in again. Continue this pattern every five minutes for one hour, then ten minutes the next hour, and so on.

◁ PACIFIERS
A pacifier can help calm and comfort a newborn or older baby when agitated.

91 DIVIDING NIGHT & DAY SLEEP

Make a distinction between how you treat day- and nighttime sleep to teach your baby there is a time for play, and a time for sleep.

- Use a bassinet or carriage for daytime naps.
- During daytime naps make sure that she is covered but not swaddled or tightly tucked in.
- Allow her two hours' nap in the day, then wake her. Give her time to adjust to waking before play or food.
- Save the crib for nighttime sleep, making it part of the bedtime routine, so that she comes to associate that place with sleep.
- At night swaddle her firmly and tuck her in. Keep lighting dim.
- At night when she wakes, pick her up, feed and change her diaper if needed, making very little fuss.

92 WHY BABIES CRY & HOW TO SOOTHE THEM

Crying is the only way babies have of telling you they are hungry or thirsty, or of getting your attention. They don't cry for the heck of it. They also cry when they are tired, and sometimes when they wake up. You will learn to recognize certain types of crying, from out-and-out colic screaming (*see p.63*) to nighttime complaining. In either case you should always respond quickly but without a lot of fuss. The following hints may help:

- Feed him, especially a newborn who will cry even if he has been fed only an hour before.
- Give him a sippy cup of water.
- Comfort him closely in your arms.
- Give him something to suck, such as a finger or pacifier.
- Rock him rhythmically and horizontally in your arms.
- Sing and talk to him.
- Change his diaper.
- Hold him upright over your shoulder and rub his back. He may be suffering from gas.
- Lay your baby on his stomach across your lap.
- Walk around the room holding him upright in your arms. Some babies respond well to this motion.
- Swaddle a small baby in a blanket to make him feel secure.
- Distract him with a mobile, hand puppet, or any bright object.
- Let him sit with you for a while while he calms down.
- Carry him in a front pack: he will be reassured by your closeness.

◁ **OTHER CAUSES OF CRYING**
Babies also cry if their surroundings are too hot or cold, or in reaction to your moods.

93 HOW TO COMFORT & REASSURE A NEWBORN

Very young babies are vulnerable to sudden loud noises, bangs, disturbances, and bright lights and will wake as a result. But newborns will almost always respond to feeling safe and secure wrapped in a blanket or cuddled in a warm embrace. They also have a strong desire for sleep, which is to your advantage. The best ways to soothe your newborn are shown below. Bear in mind that gentle motion and gentle sounds are your best resources: swinging, rocking, swaying, walking, and dancing while holding the baby provide this perfectly. So does the motion of a vehicle – but only as a last resort!

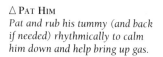

Use a rattle toy to keep his attention

△ PAT HIM
Pat and rub his tummy (and back if needed) rhythmically to calm him down and help bring up gas.

Hold him under his bottom

△ HUG HIM
Hold your baby upright against your shoulder. He will feel secure and will be comforted by the familiar beat of your heart. Always support his head with your hand.

Share feeding with a bottle

△ BOTTLE-FEED
The best way to soothe him in the first months is to feed him. With bottle-feeding Dad can share the duties and give Mom a break.

Rock Steady ▷
*Sing her lullabies
while rocking her
on her back in this
position. Jig up and
down by shifting from
foot to foot, and vary
the pace of the
rocking.*

△ Breast-Feed
*The most likely reason for
crying is hunger. Frequent
breast-feedings day and night
will give him food, suckling,
and comfort all rolled into one.*

*Make eye
contact to let
him know
you're there*

*Firm support
from your arms
and hands*

*A postcard
or picture
book can
catch his eye*

△ Distract your Baby
*Your baby may forget why he is crying
for a while if you distract his attention
with a bright or noisy toy. You can also
pick him up and point out things in the
room to help soothe him.*

94 Coping with a Colicky Baby

A baby who cries inconsolably
for two or three hours a day,
usually in the early evening,
may have colic. Colic usually
develops by three weeks and
disappears by about three
months. It is distressing, but
not harmful. All you can do is
comfort your baby by holding,
rocking, or rubbing his tummy.
Sucking often soothes him.

BABY HEALTH & SAFETY

95 READING YOUR BABY'S TEMPERATURE

A rectal reading gives the most accurate check, or you can tuck the bulb of a mercury thermometer into your baby's armpit for a few minutes. Normal temperature for a baby is 96.8°–99.5° F (36°–37.5° C). If it rises over 100° F (38° C) this may be a sign of illness. If it is still raised after resting for 30 minutes check for symptoms: Is she shivering? Does she feel hot? Check her forehead with your cheek, not your hand, to feel how hot she is. Call your doctor if she is under 12 months, and has a temperature over 101° F (38.3° C); or has a fever for over 24 hours.

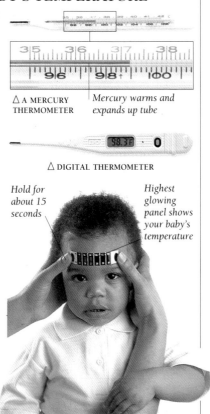

△ A MERCURY THERMOMETER

Mercury warms and expands up tube

△ DIGITAL THERMOMETER

Hold for about 15 seconds

Highest glowing panel shows your baby's temperature

Dual Celsius and Fahrenheit scale

Temperature panel reading glows

°F	95	96.8	98.5	100.4	102.2	104
°C	35	36	37	38	39	40

△ FOREHEAD THERMOMETER

SIMPLE TEMPERATURE SCANNING ▷
Less accurate than mercury thermometers, but easy to use, the strip thermometer can indicate a raised temperature. Press it flat on the baby's forehead with your thumbs.

96 GIVING MEDICINE

Put a bib on your baby because medicines are often sticky, the baby is likely to wriggle, and spillage will occur. Have some wipes or a wet washcloth close at hand to wipe clean. Always follow the instructions to the letter, and use a 1 tsp (5 ml) medicine spoon or dropper. If your baby cannot yet sit up, hold him as if you were going to feed him. Tilt the dropper or spoon slightly, letting the medicine fall straight into his mouth. If this does not work, let him suck the medicine off your fingertip as you dip from a measured dose in a spoon.

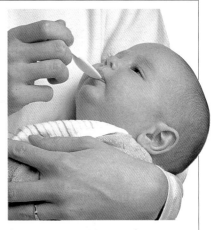

△ SPOON-FEEDING MEDICINE
Cradle a young baby as if feeding, with his head tilted back in your arm.

97 GETTING RID OF CRADLE CAP

Cradle cap appears as brown, crusty patches on a baby's head. Rub the scales with baby oil to soften them. Leave the oil on for 12 to 24 hours, then comb his hair gently with a very fine comb to loosen the scales. Finally wash his hair – most of the scales will wash away. If it spreads to the baby's face, body, or diaper area, producing a red, scaly rash, ask your pediatrician to recommend a suitable ointment. Do not use soap, baby lotion, or baby bath on these areas.

Rub oil onto the affected area

RUB FLAKES AWAY ▷
Cradle cap looks unattractive, but it generally does not do any harm.

98 GETTING RID OF CONJUNCTIVITIS

This is a very common, mild eye infection, where the eyelashes stick together after sleep or pus gets in the corner of the eye. Clean your baby's eyes twice a day with cotton balls dipped in warm water that has been boiled. Call the doctor if it does not clear up in three days.

△ COTTON BALL CLEAN
Wipe each eye outward from the inner corner with fresh damp cotton.

99 SEEKING HELP

It is not always easy to tell if a young baby is very ill, so always follow your instincts. If you are at all worried, call your doctor straight away if baby:
- Cries more than usual, or his crying sounds different from usual for over an hour.
- Seems drowsy, listless, unusually quiet, or restless.
- Refuses two feedings or does not demand a feeding in six hours.

100 SAFETY AT HOME

You can minimize the risk of accidents in the home if you take simple safety precautions.
- Place bouncy chairs, Moses baskets, and bassinets on the floor, away from open doors, fires, or tabletops. Remove all sharp objects.
- Place special covers over unused electrical wall sockets.
- Keep table lamps, telephones, and all cords out of reach.
- Use place mats rather than a tablecloth that baby could pull.
- Install gates at the bottom and top of stairs, and a gate across the kitchen door, before baby crawls.
- Keep a first aid kit on hand.

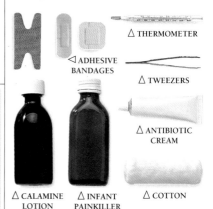

△ THERMOMETER

◁ ADHESIVE BANDAGES

△ TWEEZERS

△ ANTIBIOTIC CREAM

△ CALAMINE LOTION   △ INFANT PAINKILLER   △ COTTON

△ FIRST AID KIT
Keep a kit filled with bandages, dressings, adhesive bandages, antibiotic cream, and ointment for cuts and grazes. Scissors and tweezers are good for extracting splinters.

KITCHEN SAFETY ▽
Keep babies away from the cooking area. Keep all sharp objects and hot items well back from work surfaces.

Guard around cooking surface; pan handle turned away

Child-resistant latches on drawers

Coiled cords reduce risk of baby grabbing

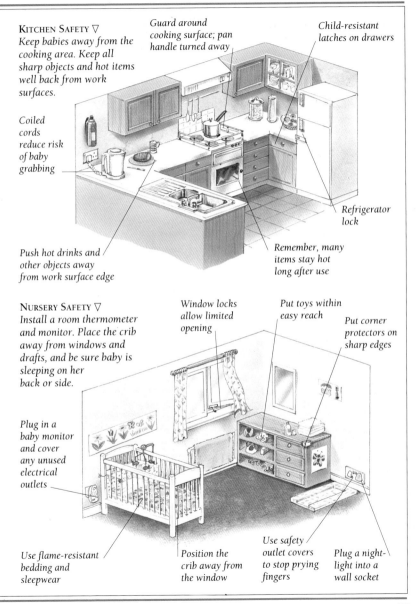

Refrigerator lock

Push hot drinks and other objects away from work surface edge

Remember, many items stay hot long after use

NURSERY SAFETY ▽
Install a room thermometer and monitor. Place the crib away from windows and drafts, and be sure baby is sleeping on her back or side.

Window locks allow limited opening

Put toys within easy reach

Put corner protectors on sharp edges

Plug in a baby monitor and cover any unused electrical outlets

Use flame-resistant bedding and sleepwear

Position the crib away from the window

Use safety outlet covers to stop prying fingers

Plug a night-light into a wall socket

101 LEARNING & DEVELOPMENT

Your baby needs your stimulation and responsiveness to develop and learn. He gets that through play, so do not separate play from the rest of the daily routine. Everything should be a game – from unpacking the groceries or making the bed to cooking meals. In the first six months he will be largely stationary but will wave his arms and kick his legs. Respond to his facial expressions with plenty of vocal encouragement and close contact. First toys, like a rattle, can be very stimulating. In the second six months he will sit up with no support, start to crawl, and may even toddle around. He will also put anything in his mouth, so be wary.

◁▽ **FIRST SIX MONTHS**
Learning to roll over is a great milestone of movement for your baby. Show and tell him how clever he is to achieve this. Always be careful not to leave him alone on a bed or other high surface.

Encourage leg kicking, especially at bathtime or when changing a diaper

Respond to his looks and arm movements

Face him at eye level so he supports his head and looks up

Let him struggle to do it himself, but give him all the encouragement you can

Once he can roll he will learn to slide forward

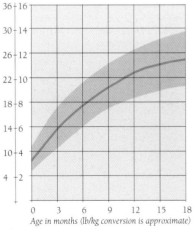

◁ **SITTING UP**
He will lean slightly forward with legs splayed out and straight. Put a cushion behind him for support.

CRAWLING ▷
Getting about and moving on all fours is a great achievement. Some babies go straight to walking without crawling.

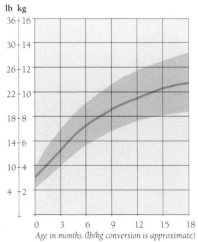

△ **CLIMBING UP**
At around seven to ten months he may be able to pull himself up. Check that there is nothing unstable in his grasp.

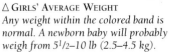

lb kg

36┼16	
30┼14	
26┼12	
22┼10	
18┼8	
14┼6	
10┼4	
4 ┼2	

0   3   6   9   12   15   18
Age in months (lb/kg conversion is approximate)

lb kg

36┼16	
30┼14	
26┼12	
22┼10	
18┼8	
14┼6	
10┼4	
4 ┼2	

0   3   6   9   12   15   18
Age in months (lb/kg conversion is approximate)

△ **GIRLS' AVERAGE WEIGHT**
Any weight within the colored band is normal. A newborn baby will probably weigh from 5½–10 lb (2.5–4.5 kg).

△ **BOYS' AVERAGE WEIGHT**
Boys, as well as girls, are likely to double their weight in the first six months. Any weight within the band is normal.

INDEX

ACKNOWLEDGMENTS

Dorling Kindersley would like to thank Hilary Bird for compiling the index, Isobel Holland for proofreading, Amelia Freeman for design assistance, Eleanor Rudd for additional modeling, and Mark Bracey for computer assistance.

Photography
KEY: t *top*; b *bottom*; c *center*; l *left*; r *right*
All photographs by Susanna Price except for: Dave King 16, 24, 25, 26 (t), 35 (bl), 37, 38 (bl), 39, 40, 41, (tr), 43 (cl), 46, 47 (t, bl), 48 (br), 49, 59 (b), 60 (t), 61, 62 (cr); Antonia Deutsch 32 (b), 33, 34 (t), 35 (br); Ray Moller 27, 38 (tr, cr, br), 41 (b), 42 (b); Jules Selmes 20, 35 (t), 56 (tr), 62 (bl, br); Steve Shott 52, 56 (cl).

Illustrations
Chris Forsey 67.